Generative AI with Large Language Models: A Comprehensive Guide

Contents

Part 1: Foundational Concepts

Welcome to the exciting world of Generative AI! This section will equip you with the essential knowledge to understand how machines are learning to generate entirely new content, from text and code to images and music. We'll break down the core principles of generative AI, delve into the fascinating world of Large Language Models (LLMs), and explore the broader category of Foundation Models (FMs) of which LLMs are a part.

Chapter 1: Generative AI Fundamentals

What is Generative AI? In this chapter, we'll unveil the magic behind generative AI. We'll explore how it differs from traditional AI and delve into its core principles. You'll learn how generative models can be trained on massive datasets to "learn" the underlying patterns and relationships within that data. This empowers them to not just analyze existing information, but to create entirely new and original content, like generating realistic images from text descriptions or composing novel musical pieces.

We'll discuss different types of generative models, such as Variational Autoencoders (VAEs) and Generative Adversarial Networks (GANs), and explore how they work at a high level.

Core Principles of Generative Models:

Here, we'll shed light on the fundamental concepts that underpin generative AI. We'll explore concepts like probabilistic modeling, where the model learns the probability of different elements occurring together, and adversarial training, where two models compete against each other to improve their capabilities.

Understanding these core principles will

equip you with a solid foundation for grasping

the inner workings of LLMs and FMs.

Chapter 2: Unveiling Large Language Models (LLMs)

Demystifying LLMs: Get ready to dive deep

into the world of Large Language Models!

This chapter will unpack what LLMs are and

what makes them special. We'll explore their

key characteristics, such as their massive size and ability to process vast amounts of text data. You'll learn how LLMs are trained on gigantic datasets of books,

articles, code, and other forms of text, allowing them to grasp complex relationships between words and sentences.

Capabilities and Applications of LLMs: Here, we'll delve into the remarkable capabilities of LLMs. We'll explore how they can be used for a wide range of tasks, including generating different creative text formats like poems, code, scripts, and even translating languages. You'll discover the immense potential of LLMs in various applications, from revolutionizing machine translation to assisting with content creation.

Limitations and Challenges of LLMs: No technology is perfect, and LLMs are no exception. We'll discuss some of the limitations and challenges associated with these powerful models. This might include potential biases present in the training data, the difficulty in interpreting how LLMs arrive at their outputs, and the computational resources required for training and running them.

Chapter 3: Foundation Models (FMs) - A Broader Perspective

The Rise of Foundation Models: This chapter broadens the horizon by introducing Foundation Models (FMs). We'll explore how LLMs fit within the larger category of FMs, which encompass a wider range of models trained on different types of data, not just text. You'll discover how FMs like vision models can analyze and generate images, while multimodal models can handle combinations of text, images, and other data types.

The Power and Impact of FMs: Here, we'll discuss the transformative power and impact of Foundation Models. We'll explore how FMs are accelerating progress in various fields, from scientific discovery to creative industries. You'll gain insights into how FMs are changing the way we approach tasks and problems, paving the way for a future filled with exciting possibilities.

This first part has equipped you with the foundational knowledge to understand generative AI, LLMs, and FMs. Now, we'll delve deeper into the specifics of LLM training, explore how to fine-tune them for specific tasks, and uncover the real-world applications that are shaping our world!

Part 2: LLMs and Generative AI Applications

Now that we have a solid understanding of LLMs and Foundation Models, let's delve into the exciting world of their applications! This section will explore how LLMs are trained, fine-tuned for specific tasks, and ultimately used to generate entirely new content and revolutionize various fields.

Chapter 4: Demystifying LLM Training

Data Acquisition and Preprocessing for LLM Training

Imagine building a house – you need solid materials to construct a strong foundation. Similarly, training LLMs requires a vast amount of high-quality data. This data could be text scraped from the internet, books, articles, code repositories, and more. The quality and diversity of this data are crucial for LLM success.

However, raw data isn't enough. Before feeding it to the LLM, preprocessing steps are necessary. This might involve cleaning the data by removing errors or inconsistencies, formatting it into a consistent structure, and potentially filtering out irrelevant information.

Training Techniques for LLMs

Once the data is prepped, it's time for the real magic – training the LLM! Here, we'll explore two main training techniques:

Supervised Learning: This approach is like having a teacher guide the LLM. We provide the model with labeled data, where each piece of data has a clear example of the desired output. For example, the LLM might be trained on pairs of English sentences and their French translations, allowing it to "learn" the patterns of translation.

Unsupervised Learning: Here, the LLM is like a curious student exploring on its own. We provide the model with vast amounts of unlabeled data, and it discovers patterns and relationships within that data on its own. This can be useful for tasks like text summarization, where the LLM learns to identify the key points of a document without

needing pre-labeled examples.

Challenges and Best Practices in LLM Training

Training LLMs is no easy feat. Challenges include:

Computational Resources: Training these massive models requires significant computing power, making it resource-intensive. **Data Biases:** If the training data is biased, the LLM can perpetuate those biases in its outputs. Mitigating bias is crucial for responsible AI development. **Overfitting:** The LLM might memorize the training data too well and struggle with unseen examples. Techniques like regularization can help prevent this.

Best practices for LLM training include:

Using High-Quality Diverse Data: The more diverse and representative the data, the better the LLM's performance. **Regularization Techniques:** These methods help prevent overfitting and ensure the LLM generalizes well to new data. **Continuous Monitoring and Evaluation:** Monitoring the training process and evaluating the LLM's performance throughout helps ensure it's learning effectively.

Chapter 5: Fine-Tuning LLMs for Targeted Tasks

Imagine a talented musician who can play various instruments. LLMs are similar - they have a broad base of knowledge but may need specific training to excel at a particular task. This is where fine-tuning comes in.

What is Fine-Tuning and Why is it Important for LLMs?

Fine-tuning is like taking that talented musician and giving them specialized training on a specific instrument, say, the violin. Here, we take a pre-

trained LLM and further train it on a specific dataset
tailored to the desired task.

For example, we could fine-tune an LLM for writing
different creative text formats like poems or code by
training it on a dataset of existing poems or code
snippets. This allows the LLM to learn the nuances of
that specific domain and generate outputs tailored to
it.

**Fine-Tuning Techniques for Different Generative
Tasks**

There are various fine-tuning techniques depending
on the desired outcome:

Text Generation: Techniques like prompting and temperature control can guide the LLM towards specific styles or topics when generating creative text formats.

Code Completion: Fine-tuning on code repositories allows the LLM to predict the next line of code based on the existing code, assisting programmers.

Machine Translation: Fine-tuning on parallel datasets of text in two languages allows the LLM to translate between those languages more accurately.

Evaluating the Performance of Fine-Tuned LLMs

Once an LLM is fine-tuned, it's crucial to evaluate its performance. This could involve human evaluation, where experts assess the quality and relevance of the LLM's outputs. Additionally, we can use automated metrics specific to the task, like BLEU score for machine translation, to gauge the LLM's effectiveness.

Text Generation and Language Processing:

> **Creative Writing:** Imagine writer's block vanishing! LLMs can be fine-tuned to generate different creative text formats, from poems and scripts to musical lyrics. They can spark inspiration, help overcome writer's block, or even co-create content with human

writers.

Machine Translation: Breaking down language barriers! LLMs are revolutionizing machine translation by offering more accurate and natural-sounding translations compared to traditional methods. This fosters communication and collaboration across cultures.

Content Creation: Boosting productivity and creativity! LLMs can be used to generate different kinds of content, from social media posts and product descriptions to news articles and marketing copy. This allows businesses and individuals to create engaging content efficiently.

Chatbots and Virtual Assistants: Having a conversation with a machine! LLMs are powering advanced chatbots and virtual assistants that can hold natural conversations, answer questions informatively, and even provide customer service.

Code Generation and Programming Assistance:

Automating Repetitive Tasks: Freeing programmers for more complex work! LLMs can automate repetitive coding tasks like generating boilerplate code or suggesting code completions. This improves programmer efficiency and reduces errors.

Learning to Code More Easily: Making coding more accessible! LLMs can be used to create interactive tutorials

or personalized learning experiences, making it easier for beginners to learn coding concepts.

Drug Discovery and Material Science Applications:

Accelerating Scientific Research: Unlocking new possibilities! LLMs can analyze massive scientific datasets to identify patterns and potential drug candidates or new materials with desired properties. This can significantly accelerate scientific discovery.

Generative AI in Content Creation:

Image Generation: Bringing ideas to life!

LLMs can be used to generate realistic images based on text descriptions. This could be used for creating illustrations, product mockups, or even generating concept art for movies and video games.

Music Composition: Composing like a maestro! LLMs can be used to generate new music pieces in different

styles or even collaborate with human composers to create unique musical experiences.

These are just a few examples, and the potential applications of generative AI are constantly expanding. As LLM technology evolves and becomes more accessible, we can expect even more innovative

and transformative applications to emerge across

various industries, shaping the future of how we

work, create, and interact with the world around us.

Part 3: Advanced Topics

Now that we've explored the fundamentals of LLMs and their applications, let's delve deeper into the technical aspects and considerations surrounding this cutting-edge technology. This section will equip you with a deeper understanding of LLM architectures, the challenges of scaling generative AI, and the importance of safety and ethics in its development and deployment.

Chapter

7: Deep Dive into LLM Architectures

Tr

an

sf

or

m

er

N

et

w

or

ks:

Th

e

Ba

ck

bo

ne

of

M

od

er

n

LL

M

s

Imagine a bustling city where information flows

freely between different districts. This is analogous

to how Transformer

networks operate. These are the architectural

workhorses powering modern LLMs, excelling at processing and understanding long sequences of text. Unlike traditional RNNs, transformers can analyze all parts of a sentence simultaneously, allowing them to grasp complex relationships between words, regardless of their position in the sequence. This leads to a deeper understanding of context and meaning within text.

Attention Mechanisms and their Role in LLM Processing

Within the Transformer network lies a crucial component called the attention mechanism. Think of it as a spotlight in a theater. The attention mechanism directs the LLM's focus to the most relevant parts of a sequence when processing information. For instance, when analyzing the sentence "The cat chased the mouse across the green field," the attention mechanism might focus on the words "cat" and "mouse" to understand the action, while also attending to "green field" to establish the setting. This selective focus allows the LLM to grasp the nuances of language more effectively.

Exploring Different LLM Architectures (e.g., GPT-3, Jurassic-1 Jumbo)

Just like different car models exist, there are various LLM architectures, each with its own strengths and weaknesses. Here are some prominent examples:

GPT-3 (Generative Pre-trained Transformer 3): This is a powerful LLM developed by OpenAI, known for its impressive text generation capabilities and ability to perform various tasks like writing different kinds of creative content and translating languages.

Jurassic-1 Jumbo: Developed by AI21 Labs, this LLM boasts a massive size and excels at tasks requiring factual accuracy and knowledge retrieval.

It's important to note that these are just a few examples, and the field of LLM architectures is constantly evolving.

Chapter 8: Scaling Generative AI: Challenges and Solutions

Computational Requirements for Training Large LLMs

Imagine trying to build a skyscraper with basic tools.

Training massive LLMs faces a similar challenge – it requires immense computational resources. These models have billions or even trillions of parameters, and training them necessitates significant computing power and vast amounts of data. This can be a hurdle for smaller organizations or individual researchers.

Techniques for Efficient LLM Training (e.g., model parallelism, distributed training)

Fortunately, advancements are being made to address these challenges. Here are some techniques for efficient LLM training:

Model Parallelism: This approach divides the

LLM model into smaller chunks, each trained on separate processors. This allows for faster training by utilizing multiple computing resources simultaneously.

Distributed Training: Similar to model parallelism, this technique distributes the training data across multiple machines, enabling faster training by processing information in parallel.

Hardware and Infrastructure Considerations for Scaling Generative AI

The hardware and infrastructure used play a crucial role in scaling generative AI. Here are some key considerations:

GPUs (Graphics Processing Units): These specialized processors are particularly adept at handling the complex calculations involved in LLM training.

TPUs (Tensor Processing Units): These custom-designed chips from companies like Google are optimized for AI workloads, offering even greater efficiency in training massive LLMs.

Cloud Computing Platforms: Cloud platforms like Google Cloud AI Platform or Amazon SageMaker offer pre-configured infrastructure and access to powerful computing resources, making LLM training more accessible to a wider range of users.

C

h

a

p

t

e

r

9

:

S

a

f

e

t

y

a

n

d

Ethics in Gene

r

a

t

i

v

e

A

l

P

o

t

e

n

t

i

a

l

B

i

a

s

e

s

a

n

d

Fairness

Conce

r

n

s

i

n

L

L

M

s

Remember the saying "garbage in, garbage out"? It applies to LLMs as well. If the training data is biased, the LLM can perpetuate those biases in its outputs. This raises concerns about fairness and the potential for discrimination. For example, an LLM trained on biased datasets might generate content that reinforces gender stereotypes or promotes offensive language.

Mitigating Risks of Generative AI (e.g., deepfakes, malicious content generation)

Generative AI also presents potential risks, like the creation of deepfakes – highly realistic, manipulated videos or audio recordings. These could be used for malicious purposes like spreading misinformation or damaging reputations. Additionally, LLMs could be used to generate malicious content, such as hate speech or spam.

Ethical Guidelines for Developing and Deploying Generative AI Systems

Following up on the potential risks of generative AI, it's crucial to establish ethical guidelines for its development and deployment. Here are some key considerations:

Transparency and Explainability: We should strive to understand how LLMs arrive at their outputs. This allows for identifying and mitigating potential biases and ensuring the generated content is reliable and trustworthy.

Fairness and Mitigating Bias: Training data needs to be carefully curated to minimize biases and ensure the LLM's outputs are fair and inclusive. Techniques like data augmentation and filtering can help achieve this.

User Privacy and Security: Protecting user data is paramount. LLMs should be developed and deployed in a way that safeguards user privacy and prevents misuse of sensitive information.

Accountability and Human Oversight: Ultimately, humans should be accountable for the development and use of generative AI systems. Human oversight is essential to ensure these systems are used responsibly and ethically.

Looking Ahead: The Future of Generative AI

The field of generative AI is rapidly evolving, holding immense potential to revolutionize various aspects of our lives. As we continue to develop and refine LLMs, addressing the ethical considerations and ensuring responsible use will be crucial. By prioritizing safety, fairness, and transparency, we can harness the power of generative AI to create a better future for all.

Here are some additional points you might consider including at the end of this section:

- Briefly discuss potential future applications of generative AI in fields like education, healthcare, and entertainment.
- Emphasize the importance of ongoing research and collaboration between researchers, developers, and policymakers to ensure the ethical and responsible development of generative AI.

This concludes Part 3 of your exploration into the fascinating world of generative AI and LLMs. I hope this content provides a comprehensive and informative overview of these groundbreaking technologies!

Part 4: The Future

Generative AI is a rapidly evolving field brimming with potential. In this final section, we'll peer into the future, exploring emerging trends, the impact of generative AI on society, and the considerations we need to address for responsible development.

Chapter 10: The Evolving Landscape of Generative AI

Emerging Trends and Advancements in LLM Research

The world of LLMs is constantly pushing boundaries. Here are some exciting trends to watch:

Even Larger and More Capable LLMs:

Researchers are striving to build even larger and more powerful LLMs, capable of handling even more complex tasks and generating even more impressive outputs.

Explainable AI: Efforts are underway to develop methods for understanding how LLMs arrive at their outputs. This will enhance transparency and trust in these models.

Multimodal LLMs: These next-generation models will not only handle text but also integrate other data modalities like images, audio, and even video. Imagine an LLM that can generate a story, compose a soundtrack, and create accompanying visuals!

The Future of Foundation Models and their Capabilities

Foundation Models represent a paradigm shift in AI. As they evolve, we can expect:

Improved Generalization: Future Foundation Models will excel at adapting to new situations and performing well on tasks they haven't been specifically trained for.

Lifelong Learning: Imagine models that can continuously learn and improve over time, just like humans. This is a future aspiration for Foundation Models.

Unlocking Scientific Mysteries: These models could become powerful research assistants, aiding scientists in analyzing complex data and accelerating breakthroughs in various fields.

Potential Applications of Generative AI in Unforeseen Areas

The potential applications of generative AI are vast and constantly expanding. Here are some unforeseen areas where it might make a splash:

Personalized Education: Imagine AI tutors tailoring learning experiences to individual students' needs and learning styles.

Personalized Healthcare: Generative AI could analyze medical data to predict and prevent diseases or even personalize treatment plans for patients.

Augmented Creativity: These models could assist artists, musicians, and designers by generating new ideas, sparking inspiration, and collaborating on creative endeavors.

Chapter 11: The Impact of Generative AI on Society

Societal and Economic Implications of Generative AI

The impact of generative AI will be felt across various aspects of society:

Transformation of Industries: Generative AI will automate tasks across various industries, potentially leading to job displacement in some sectors. However, it will also create new opportunities in areas like AI development and data science.

Shifting Skillsets: The future workforce will likely require a blend of technical skills and human-centric qualities like creativity, critical thinking, and problem-solving.

Accessibility and Democratization of Knowledge: Generative AI has the potential to make information and knowledge more accessible to everyone, bridging the gap between information haves and have-nots.

The Future of Work and the Role of Generative AI

As automation through generative AI increases, the nature of work will inevitably change. Here's what to consider:

Human-AI Collaboration: The future of

work might involve humans and AI working together, leveraging each other's strengths. Humans can provide strategic direction and creativity, while AI can handle routine tasks and complex data analysis.

Reskilling and Upskilling: Equipping the workforce with the necessary skills to thrive in an AI-driven future will be crucial. Continuous learning and upskilling will be essential.

Ethical Considerations for Job Automation: The potential for job displacement through automation raises ethical concerns. Measures should be taken to ensure a smooth transition for workers whose jobs might be affected.

Regulatory Considerations and Policy Frameworks for Generative AI

As generative AI continues to evolve, robust policies and regulations will be needed to ensure its responsible development and use. Here are some key areas for consideration:

> **Bias and Fairness:** Regulations should be in place to mitigate bias in training data and ensure fair and inclusive outcomes from generative AI systems.

> **Data Privacy and Security:** User data privacy

needs to be protected. Regulations should ensure responsible data collection, storage, and usage practices.

Transparency and Explainability: Developing frameworks that promote transparency in how generative AI systems work will be crucial for building public trust.

By addressing these considerations and fostering international collaboration, we can ensure that generative AI progresses for the benefit of all.

This concludes Part 4, marking the end of your exploration into the exciting world of generative AI. Remember, this is just the beginning. As generative AI continues to evolve, the possibilities are truly limitless. Let's embrace the future with a blend of curiosity, responsibility, and a commitment to using

this technology for the betterment of humanity.

www.ingramcontent.com/pod-product-compliance
Lightning Source LLC
LaVergne TN
LVHW051614050326
832903LV00033B/4490